Introduction

Any business decision that must be made today can be daunting – but none more so than the decision to expand or move your business location. The moving process is multi-faceted, complex and involves every aspect of your business as well as every one of your employees. If your business is small, you may find yourself without the necessary personnel you'll need to make the move seamlessly and without a negative impact on your bottom line. And if your business is large – the task can be so complex and formidable to be nearly overwhelming. No matter the size of your company, businesses need to plan ahead and consider all their options in order to reduce problems, save time and money.

Each step in the decision to move - preplanning, budgeting and then the actual move itself - has a number of serious and potentially business-altering points to be considered. This book will make it much easier on you and your relocation crew, as we present the Top Business Relocation Tips. There are many things that can derail your plans and best intentions, cost you time and money you didn't need to spend, and expose you to unnecessary obligations and liabilities. The following tips are based on many years of experience; they'll cover the most important issues and will help you save time and money as well as provide you with a guide that will make your move nearly stress-free.

Table of Contents

Table of Contents

Table of Contents

The 3 P's of Relocation

Before we begin, the most effective business moves adhere to the 3 P's of relocation:

1. **Planning** - your office move will need a framework to help you effectively manage your move. Planning is one of those business functions that is too often overlooked, the lack of which causes the collapse of whatever it is that you're trying to accomplish. Make sure you put together a plan and a RELOCATION PLANNING COMMITTEE so that no one individual becomes responsible for everything and so you can categorize and delegate the most important functions and jobs. The tips below are divided into certain relocation stages, making it easier for you to follow: A) BEFORE THE MOVE, B) DURING THE MOVE and C) AFTER THE MOVE.

2. **Preparation** – each step in your relocation process requires preparation. What does the relocation process require and what resources are needed to prepare for that particular step? The following tips will help make your preparation more thorough so you won't accidentally overlook an important decision.

3. **Professionals** – The successful relocation of every business requires the help of relocation professionals and should be a collaborative effort between your internal relocation team and outside vendors. Individuals and companies such as tenant relocation brokers, business attorneys, CPAs, architects, interior designers, IT and Telecom specialists, movers, construction crews, and others should be considered to be hired as part of your relocation team. Engage these outside vendors as early in the relocation process as possible. These professionals have the most relocation experience and can help you save time and money in the long run.

BEFORE THE MOVE

TIP #1

The Critical Question:
Why are you moving?

In order to answer this question you'll want to determine the basis for your move. Ask yourself, "Why are we moving?" and consider the following questions:

✓ Are you breaking your lease for some reason? Is your lease expiring? Is your business expanding, contracting or consolidating?

✓ Do you need to reduce overhead?

✓ Do you want to be closer to customers?

✓ Do you want to be closer to your vendors or your shipping & freight facilities?

Answering this question will help you determine how to deal with your current obligations and potential liabilities. Do you have an existing lease? Can you get out of it? Do you have to give notice?

Depending on the intricacies of your situation, you may want to consider hiring a **real estate attorney** to help advise you as you wrestle with these decisions (http://www.lawyers.com).

☷ TIP #2

Make Sure You are Moving
to the "Right" Location

There are hundreds of factors to consider when deciding where to relocate your business. A few factors to consider include:

Location - Does your business benefit from being in a particular neighborhood? If so, will it be worth it to you to pay a higher rent to access higher levels of foot traffic? For example, if you sell high-end women's shoes, would it make sense for you to move to a higher income area where residents can afford your goods?

Target Market - Who is your target market and can they be targeted on a geographic basis? If so, would your company benefit by moving to a different area of town or a different city or state in order to be closer to your customer base?

Population – Is it better for your business to be in a major metropolitan market or does the product or service you offer lend itself to a suburban or rural surrounding?

Economic base – If your business interacts with the local community (in the way that a restaurant or dry cleaner may), you'll need to consider the income levels, unemployment numbers and other economic factors in your potential new office areas.

Your competitors - Perhaps all your competition is in a certain area of the country and there would be a level of prestige your company would gain just by being close to those vendors? For example, if your company is in a "high tech" industry, you may improve your company's positioning by moving to an area like Silicon Valley in California.

TIP #2

The size of the market – If your business depends on foot traffic, it would be important to consider the demographic profile of the neighborhood you are considering moving into. Are there enough consumers in your target market in the particular neighborhood you're looking at?

Pricing – Think about your cash flow – does your business model allow for you to spend that much money for a rental location? If you can increase sales by gaining valuable traffic in your target market, the answer to that may be yes.

Employee availability & skillset – Does your business require highly skilled or educated laborers? If so make sure the neighborhood you move to can supply you with qualified employees.

Current and future market trends – Be sure to consider the short and long term urban plans for your new neighborhood. You may not be happy to find that a big anchor store is moving out of the complex you just moved into, for example.

The neighborhood – Spend some time in that neighborhood - don't just drive through the area with your realtor; go shopping there or have dinner at a local restaurant. Get a feel for what type of people live and work there to make sure it's right for you and your company,

Utilities – Depending on the area you move into and the building you choose, you may have to pay for electricity rather than having it bundled into your lease. Moving into an area that has been deregulated can save you a ton of cash. If available, be sure you have a smart meter installed for maximum savings!

Voice & Data Circuits – This is a very commonly over looked item. Sure all buildings will have these services, however all services are not created equally.

TIP #2

Here are a few voice & data issues to research:

Bandwidth - Do you know how much bandwidth you need?

Existing contracts & penalties - if you are under contract with a provider and moving into an area that they do not service, you could be facing cancellation fees. This is another issue that you should consider when reviewing the costs of your move.

Customers – You should also consider the impact that relocating will have on your current customers. Will they be willing to travel to you? If you are in the service industry and you need to be present at your clients' premises to carry out your business, will it still be financially viable for you to do so?

Deregulation - Are you in a deregulated area? If not, your service rate over the time you are in this new location could cost your THOUSANDS of dollars more. Even worse, you could be stuck with this provider for a very long time.

TIP #3

Establish The Requirements
For Your New Space

Have your planning committee decide what you need, what you haven't been able to do due to lack of space or the right kind of space, if you will need more space for more employees (or less), when you'll need to be in the new offices, what the key elements are that you'll need in your new space, and so forth.

You may want to consider hiring a **Tenant Relocation Specialist or Broker** to help you find a good commercial space and to help you negotiate the best lease for your needs. If you do, make sure you review these items with your tenant relocation broker:

✓ The size of office required & if you need other facilities in addition to offices (such as a warehouse, a shipping facility –with or without a dock, a lab, manufacturing facilities, etc.) For more info about how much space you'll need: https://www.thebalance.com/how-much-office-space-do-you-need-2533790.

✓ The type & length of lease required – short term leases have advantages like providing more flexibility but longer term leases provide benefits like fixed lease costs over the term of the lease.

✓ The preferred location – there are many things that a relocation specialist can help you with regarding location selection. They can help you think through your cost of goods and ultimately how that will influence your customer's pricing and if that's a smart move for you or not.

✓ The type of building(s) desired – a good relocation specialist should know the pros and cons of the various building types

TIP #3

and will help you to think about things you wouldn't normally consider.

✓ The budget for the space – the relocation expert will walk you through the basics of a budget making it easier all the way around to have someone "in the know" to help you through this process.

✓ The parking lot requirements – there's more to parking lots than how many spaces you'll get and a relocation specialist can help you negotiate the number of spaces you need, think about the longer term and issues like who'll be responsible if a big branch falls into you parking space, to name just a few. For more info on negotiation parking lot issues visit: http://www.coydavidson.com/best-practices/dont-overlook-parking-when-negotiating-your-office-lease/

✓ The timing of move – the timing of the move is something people don't always consider but a relocation specialist will know about seasonal costs and issues that will influence the decision about when is the best time to move.

You should start researching and looking for a new office facility about eight to twelve months prior to the date you'd like to relocate your business. Due to the scope of the office hunting project, anytime you're looking for a new office lease or purchase, you should be working with a professional real estate agent. Create a list of "must haves" and compare that to a list of issues you see in each of the top 3 or 4 offices you are shown that you like. Take photos of each office you see and keep track of the features that each location offers so you can discuss these items later with your relocation team.

TIP #4

Real Estate Attorneys Can Keep You Out of Trouble

When relocating, many of your decisions involve the purchase or leasing of commercial property. Because there are so many complex laws governing the commercial real estate sector, your best choice is to hire a qualified commercial real estate attorney, and/or a business attorney that has a good deal of real estate experience, particularly negotiating property leases or purchases. Commercial RE attorneys are necessary in commercial leasing situations to draft lease documents, representation in tenant disputes, and providing counsel on the purchase of commercial property. The real estate attorney will also help you in a build-out situation where you need to hire contractors to enlarge or enhance an existing location.

Ask businesses in your old and/or new area to recommend real estate attorneys for you. If you are moving a long distance, it's best to find a good attorney in the new location, although, if you are breaking a lease, you may also need one in the old location as well. If you can't find a good referral, call the local bar association in the area you are moving to and ask them to recommend some good commercial real estate attorneys for you and make sure you ask them to provide background and educational information, if complaints have been filed against them, along with other information.

TIP #5

Obtaining Economic Development Assistance

Contacting the office of economic development and chambers of commerce is a great way to get started when looking for a new office location.

These services are offered in most of the major metropolitan areas and many of the smaller to mid-sized cities and towns. They will often provide you with a great deal of information about business and tax benefits, the availability of certain types of employees and their skill levels, real estate costs, laws and business related regulations, availability of employee training programs, state healthcare services and much more information that you will find helpful when looking for your new office location.

You may even be able to acquire tax benefits & credits for each new job you import to the new area as well as free employee training programs, reduced utility fees and even discounted building rates or free office rent. Economic development groups usually have databases of real estate availability that they will give you free access to as well as many other benefits that will act as an incentive to coax you into their city.

I have worked with many companies who have found property to relocate or expand to over the years. It is mind blowing at the deals you can negotiate with motivated area representatives. So if the economic development representative for Area "A" does not offer terms that are favorable, then contact the economic development representative for Area "B". If you really want the best deal, get them bidding against each other!

TIP #6

Be Sure To Consider
Tax Issues

You might be able to lower your taxes. Moving from one location to another can sometimes reduce your tax burden. A move from one county to another can lower your sales taxes, while a move to a new state might eliminate inventory or personal income taxes. Consider how your taxes will be impacted by a move to a different city, county or state. Keep in mind that there are many states that have tax codes that are specifically crafted to entice new businesses to move to their areas. Contact the Chamber of Commerce in a potential new city or area and/or hire a Tax Attorney that practices in the new area for professional advice.

In addition to taxes, calculate your costs for licenses, permits and fees based on your current location and other locations you're considering to determine if that difference justifies a move to that particular area.

TIP #7

The Business Registration Process

It's important to remember that you'll need to reregister your business when you move to another state and if you just move from one county to another you have to notify the office of corporations so they know where to find you for tax purposes. A "DBA Declaration" may have to be filed if you own a sole proprietorship, a partnership or if you operate under a business name. In the case of an LLC or Corporation you'll want to consult with an attorney because you will need to conduct more complex steps to be able to relocate your business. For more information about these steps contact the Small Business Administration at http://www.sba.com.

There may also be business licensing issues that you'll need to update or edit depending on what your profession is (for example if you're an attorney or a CPA, your business related licensing entities will have specific applications that will be required for you to reestablish your certification at a new location). The same site above will provide you with more detailed information about any required business licenses you may need that will be issued by your new state. Visit this website at http://www.sba.com/business-resources/licenses-permits/ for more information. Depending on what county you're in, you may need a "Certificate of Occupancy" so check with your county clerk to confirm if you need this or not.

TIP #8

Changes To Your Business Organization When Moving To Another State

If you have a corporation:

If you are a corporation and plan to move your corporate offices to a new state, you have a number of choices you can make. You have these options:

✓ You can choose to keep your corporate status in the old state and register as a foreign corporation doing business in your new state. (Being a "foreign" corporation simply means that you were incorporated in another state.)

✓ You may choose to dissolve your corporation in your current (old) state and form a new corporation in the relocation state.

✓ Or, you can do a "reorganization" where you form a new corporation in the new state and merge your old corporation into the new one.

✓ Determining which of these choices is best for your company typically depends on the states involved and your short and long term goals. Think about the following:

If you keep your old corporation and register to do business in a new state, you'll end up paying 2 annual franchise taxes. A franchise tax is a tax imposed by states on corporations; it depends both on the net worth of the corporation and on its net income attributable to activities within the state. You'll need to find out what each state (old and new) will require you to pay. You will probably pay a minimum fee to your old state and another fee to the new state. In addition, you'll have to file tax returns in both states (even if you don't owe taxes in both) and you'll end up with double the accounting costs, as

TIP #8

well. You may have been incorporated in Nevada or Delaware, due to their pro-business climate and if so, you might choose to stay there, while registering as a foreign corporation in the new state. Just keep in mind that there are both State and Federal tax issues and dissolutions costs so your best bet is to hire a business or tax attorney for the best advice going forward.

If you have an LLC:

Limited liability companies have similar decisions to make, however, there are even more choices on how to handle your relocation.   For example:

- ✓ You can continue your LLC in your old state and register to do business as a foreign LLC in the relocation state.

- ✓ You can form a new LLC in the relocation state and dissolve your old LLC.

- ✓ You can form an LLC in the new state and then have the owners contribute their membership interests to it from the original LLC.

- ✓ You can merge your existing LLC into a newly formed LLC in the new state.

TIP #9

How Much Planning Time Will You Need?

Deciding how much time you will need to plan your move is certainly something that varies depending on the type of business you have, how long you've been in business, along with other factors such as the number of employees and materials that you'll need to move from the old location to the new location. Just remember that nothing can be more beneficial to your move than preplanning. As you plan, you will discover what problems may arise and be able to resolve them before they happen. Here are some guidelines that professional business relocators have developed in deciding how much time you'll really need:

✓ A small office needs about 3 to 6 months of planning prior to the move.

✓ A medium office needs about 6 to 8 months of planning prior to the move.

✓ A large office needs anywhere from 8 to 18 months of planning prior to the move.

Here's a story about the negative impact of not starting your moving plan early enough and not properly planning the timing of the move:

My firm recently had the opportunity to work with the administration of a new private school which was scheduled to open at the end of August. Unfortunately our first meeting was in the middle of July. Since this was our first meeting we went about discussing the requirements the school had to open. We began by designing the network for the school and classrooms as the curriculum was a cloud based solution. We then discussed their other needs including a VOIP system, paging, video surveillance,

access controls and most importantly, the bandwidth necessary to meet their daily requirements.

These first two hurdles were difficult to handle: first, the installation of any circuit for the necessary bandwidth would take at least 45 days, and the second was obtaining the necessary financing to complete the implementation.

As you can imagine, the end of August opening was not a realistic goal and a scaled down project was finally completed by the beginning of December. Fortunately for the school administration a church in the area allowed the school to open using their facilities but the enrollment was much less than expected. Fortunately a disaster was avoided but with more preplanning a smoother and more productive implementation could have been accomplished."

⬚ TIP #10

Assembling Your Relocation Team

Put together your in-house relocation planning committee and teams. Who at your office has the most knowledge regarding your current facility and future needs? Delegate the move to a Project Leader to manage the entire move process. This person should have enough time to dedicate to the project, have the trust of senior management and the authority to act on behalf of the company.

> **Author's Note:** The person that you choose as Project Leader, is likely to have NEVER attempted a project of this magnitude. It is my experience that a business owner rarely ever handles this him or herself rather they delegate the project to an assistant or the office manager. Knowing that this may be the first time this person has ever relocated a business (which is very different than a residential move), be patient with them. If this person is not up to the task, you will likely lose this employee following the move. Blame is placed both on the executives and on the person(s) responsible for the move. I have seen too many people FIRED or voluntarily leave a company after a fiasco of a move, so I would highly recommend hiring a professional relocation team if you don't have the right person for this job.

Be sure to develop teams who understand how your business works, can develop move strategies, and can help you stay on time and on budget. Make sure you give someone on each team the authority to complete the things that need to be done. There's no more surefire way to disaster than thinking you can handle everything yourself. Do you have employees that can help with decisions regarding IT, telecom, logistics, employee services, etc.? If so, put them in charge of relocation teams and ask for suggestions along the way.

Make sure there is one relocation team member assigned to

each department, so there is someone who can take responsibility for all the issues related to moving that one department. When you get your site maps and inventory lists completed make sure that each department relocation team member has a copy of each of these items. For smaller companies, many times there is not an opportunity to set up teams - and that is okay. However, you may need to bring in some outside professional consultants to ensure that your move goes according to plan.

TIP #11

Hiring Third-Party Vendors

Often, hiring outside companies to handle those jobs that you just can't handle yourself, or don't have the expertise to handle in-house, is your best and most cost-effective bet. Depending on the size of your company, you will probably need to hire a good Real Estate attorney, IT Specialist, Telecom planner/provider, Ad Agency, Tenant Relocation Broker, Moving Companies, General Contractor, Electricians, Interior Designers, and so forth.

Many companies try to handle some of these jobs themselves, but when they do, it usually takes considerably more time, more money and more headaches. Third party vendors are more qualified and have experience in their area of expertise that you or your employees don't possess. Ask other companies who have relocated to recommend vendors to you. You can also find good references online, making it a great place to source out vendors who do good work, on time, and with very few negative comments from businesses that have used them in the past.

My firm, Your Business Solutions, has many years of experience helping companies just like yours to handle the complexities of a business relocation. We offer a complimentary consultation to answer any of your important questions about moving. Your can learn more here: http://relocatingyourbusiness.com/free-business-relocation-consultation/

TIP #12

Introduce Your Entire Team
to the New Offices

Once you have all the relocation team member positions assigned, ask each one of them to provide tours to all the employees of the new offices while the head of the relocation team does the same with all the company executives.

> **Author's note:** You may want to encourage each department to hold a "picnic lunch" at the new site (if the new landlord permits). This not only lets your employees familiarize themselves with the facility, but it also takes advantage of the fact that employees have gathered and gives them the opportunity to develop camaraderie with each other.

By the time the move date rolls around, everyone should have been shown their new offices, how to get into the facility, where they're expected to park, where the break rooms/rest rooms are and where the postal facilities are located. Employees should also be given a map of the new offices that clearly indicates where the fire and life safety features are. Take this opportunity to distribute any other applicable information to your employees such as safety procedures, moving schedule, the start date for the new offices, parking spots/numbers and alarm codes, for example. It may be appropriate to hand out building access cards, office keys and mailbox keys at this time as well. Keep track of each employee that receives these keys so you have an accurate record of this going forward. You may want to also take this opportunity to make sure that employees have the latest "Employee Manual" because it is essential that you have a signature on file for every employee showing that they've been made aware of even the smallest policy changes. Be sure to have each employee provide you with a signature that you can keep to have a record that they've received and read this information and be sure to keep those signatures in each employee's file for future reference.

TIP #13

Include your Employees
in the Moving Process

Make sure your employees are a part of your move. Encourage your employees to participate, provide feedback and input on your company's needs and potential problems. When employees will be asked to move to another area or city, make sure they understand what the benefits & costs will be as well as communicating your relocation policy with them. If there are other options (such as telecommuting) for employees who can't or don't want to relocate, let them know what all their choices are.

Make it easier for your staff by providing them with information about the new location such as housing prices, realtor names, schools, hospitals, fitness facilities for example. Consult with each employee regarding their specific needs and issues that they'd like to see improved in the new offices. If an employee hasn't had enough space to work, now would be the time to plan for expanding their work areas. If an employee is in charge of a group of people, now would be a good time to build out an office where the manager can easily keep an eye on all his or her subordinates.

TIP #14

Arranging for the Move with Office Management at Both Locations

In order to move you'll need to make arrangements with both the old office and the new office management. If you are moving from an upper floor, you will need to reserve the freight elevator so that you have access to it during the move. This is an aspect of the move that's often overlooked and can be detrimental to your move "timeline" if your movers show up, your team is ready and the elevator is being used by another company. Make sure the elevator wall pads are in place to protect the elevator during your move – you don't want to be held responsible for a new elevator if something you do during your move damages the equipment!

In addition to this you'll need to ask both management companies if there are alleys that need to be reserved or which are restricted during certain days and/or if there are loading or warehouse docks involved you'll want to confirm that those are available and will be accessible when your movers show up. You will also want to consider the type of trucks your movers will be arriving with to confirm that they match up to any dock heights or height restrictions around the buildings you're leaving as well as the one you're moving to.

You should also make a point of checking the halls, door widths and heights, elevator sizes, stairwells and other areas of egress and entry to confirm that they will accommodate the items you're moving. If you were one of the first tenants in your old building you never knew if large pieces of furniture or art were moved in BEFORE entry ways or doors were built. In any case if there are any issues you'd want to find that out before the day of the move as opposed to finding it out while movers and helpers are standing by. You will also need to confirm the weight of your heaviest item and compare that to the weight restrictions of your elevators. That's another item that you'd want to try

to resolve before the day of the move as opposed to while the clock is ticking with your laborers.

While you are communicating with the management offices at both locations be sure and ask them if they are aware of any restrictions you should be aware of as well as any labor policies, procedures or move-in or move-out restrictions you'd need to be aware of before your moving crew arrives.

Finally ask the management at the new and old locations to be sure and turn the air-conditioning on if you'll be moving during hours when it's normally turned off. Keep track of this time as you may be billed for it and will want to ensure that the hours you're being billed for are legitimate. Also, ask for an emergency number for someone in maintenance at both facilities in case something happens during the move and the maintenance team needs to be contacted.

TIP #15

Relocation Brokers Can Save You Time & Headaches

Find a good Relocation Specialist/Broker: a business relocation consultant can provide advice to a company which is thinking about moving, helping them select a new location and making all the arrangements for the move. This can include relocating key personnel, finding local non-essential personnel, negotiating the permits process for businesses and providing other services which will help a business get back into operations quickly after a major move.

You may consider calling other firms with large offices in the area to see whom they work with, if they will share the information. Word of mouth and personal recommendations remain one of the best sources for finding the kind of help you need. You can also extend your search by contacting local Chambers of Commerce, Better Business Bureaus and other community service organizations.

TIP #16

Finding a Top Notch Business Moving Company

Moving your office can be extremely stressful – think of all the items that could potentially get lost, furniture or computers that could be damaged or broken, or business records that could become disorganized and nearly impossible to file back in their right order. For these reasons and others, finding and hiring a good commercial mover is essential to your relocation.

Delays in moving can have a serious and negative effect on your business – so all the more reason why you need to find a reputable mover who can pick up and deliver on time and have a good reputation for on-time moves. Don't hesitate to call their references to check on the commercial movers you are considering. No one can tell you better than another business owner, if the mover was honest, did a good job, was on time, and communicated with them on an ongoing basis throughout the move.

Other items to consider include:

✓ Most moving company estimators bid low to beat the competition and many provide non-binding estimates. You should ask for a **binding estimate**, which would require the moving company estimator to tell you exactly what the move will cost and usually means that the estimator will come to your office to see how much furniture you have and what else needs to be moved. Pursuant to the Federal Motor Carrier Safety Association (www.fmsca. dot.gov) a binding estimate must describe in detail what you are shipping and list all the services you are getting.

✓ The mover should know what to do in order to protect your possessions, furniture, computers, documents, and personal items. The Better Business Bureau (www.bbb. org.us) in your area may have reports about the company

TIP #16

you are thinking of using – good and bad.

✓ Make sure the movers have the dates available for your move so you don't find out later that they cannot accommodate your needs. Let them know when they should begin the move and when they must be finished. The moving date information must be specific and guaranteed.

✓ Additional things to consider about your moving company:

➤ What year did the moving company start in the moving business?

➤ Are the moving companies you're considering listed with any industry associations or the Better Business Bureau? Have you checked with your local city or state complaint bureau? (To find this Google "business complaints").

➤ Inquire about the type of insurance each company that you're considering carries. Insurance policies will either offer the value of fully replacing the lost or broken items OR they might only provide limited liability. Limited liability may only cover as little as 60 cents per pound per article. With this type of insurance, if your moving company damages your 10-pound printer that cost you $1,000, you will be reimbursed by only $6. Request that your moving company provide you with a certificate of insurance so you can call the company to confirm that the policy is in force. This may sound a bit paranoid but it doesn't hurt to be careful and to confirm that your goods are going to be fully covered.

➤ Ask your moving company to review their delivery damage claims procedures with you or one of your representatives. A legitimate company won't hesi-

tate to provide you with whatever reassurances you request to make sure you feel comfortable.

➢ Does the company you're hiring have a contact person or a "point of communications" with whom you can talk? If so have they provided you with this person's name & cell phone number from the beginning or have you had to plead for that information? Has the company you're considering hiring given you the name of a supervisor or some point of contact that can make critical, time sensitive decisions if and when you need to make changes or on the spot decisions about your move?

➢ Call the company you have decided to hire and ask a manager to perform a "walk thru" prior to the move, in order to familiarize them with the logistics and the layouts of your existing and new locations. Not only will this "walk through" reduce any last minute issues, but it will also introduce you to the person in charge and give you an opportunity to collect business contact information before the move.

➢ Look up the insurance information and licensing status of the moving companies you're considering at the FMCSA or the Federal Motor Carrier Safety Administration website (www.fmcsa.dot.gov). You can also find out how many trucks the company owns to give you an idea of the size of the company and to see if the information you've been told matches up with what is on record. The FMCSA website has a wealth of other helpful information including specifics about your rights and responsibilities.

➢ You can also check a company's ratings with the American Moving & Storage Association (www.moving.org) as well as the Better Business Bureau in your area (www.bbb.org.us).

TIP #17

Call your Insurance Company to Discuss Coverage

Contact your existing insurance company to find out what coverage you have and what that policy will cover during the move. Confirm that the policies cover all the items that are going to be moved including furniture and equipment that's owned as well as leased. Find out if your coverage covers the cars of employees that are going to be helping since you could be liable for their welfare (and the welfare of others) while they are driving between the old and new offices. If your policies are anything less than desirable, you can discuss increasing the coverage *before the move*.

Don't forget to ask your insurance rep about liability, accidental death & dismemberment as well as Worker's Compensation Insurance and tell your insurance representative the names of the employees that are going to be helping with the move so they can specifically confirm that those people are covered and your risk of liability is minimal. And of course, don't forget to add your new building to your commercial property and casualty policy and then drop the old location after your move.

TIP #18

Finding A Good General Contractor

Finding a good General Contractor is an important step when relocating your business. Many times, a business that's relocating finds a good location, but the building needs renovations to work optimally. The new location may need additional electrical work, more office spaces, conference rooms, or even bathrooms, to name just a few of the necessary potential construction projects. Developing a great relationship with a top-notch commercial contractor will help simplify the move and get you up and working much faster. To get a quote, be sure and review your overall plan and then create a budget; after that create an outline of the proposal that you can submit to a few general contractors.

"The most common problem is that people don't know what they want vs. what they need," says Michael Bellaman, President and CEO of Associated Builders and Contractors. "There's a difference. You have to be honest about that. Before selecting a contractor, the buyer has to be clear about want vs. need in terms of the service level, the scope of work they're looking for, the level of quality that they want, safety, the schedule and of course the budget." (Jane Schmitt, 2013)

The National Association of Contractors' website (Associated Builders and Contractors at www.abc.org) purports that it has nearly a hundred chapters representing tens of thousands of construction and other industry firms with close to 2 million employees. They range from small, independent operators to large industry giants with special capabilities and experience. The website also has a "Locate a Chapter" link that will direct you to state chapters where you can find information on local contractors in your area.

TIP #18

Author's Note: If you are moving into a commercial office building, most of the time the building management will highly recommend you use THEIR general contractor. However, just because the building management is recommending someone doesn't mean that you have to use them or that it's even a good idea to use them. Conduct due diligence on this contractor just as you would with any other contractor. You may discover that the "Preferred Contractor" is a friend or family member of the building owner or management team. I stopped counting how many times we have uncovered this. Do your company a huge favor and check out all contractors regardless of recommendations.

What you really need is to find a company that will deliver great services at a fair price. To find a reputable company, you may need to ask around, or do an online "recommendation" search. Call the contractors' references and be sure to ask detailed questions that relate to the precise tasks you need done. By searching the Secretary of State's website in your state, you can determine if a potential contractor has ever been involved in any lawsuits or had any disciplinary action taken against them by a licensing organization. Make sure you check their insurance certificates and determine if they carry an adequate amount of insurance for your particular job; they will need *at least* liability and worker's comp. You can also obtain a credit report on them at Dun & Bradstreet (www.dunandbradstreet.com).

Make sure you determine who is going to oversee the contractor's ongoing work and get periodic updates from them. Communication is the key to a successful renovation. Make sure your contractor is obtaining permits in a timely fashion so your project doesn't fall behind. Also, be sure your agreement with your general contractor includes a clause about scheduling (and what will happen if they do fall behind or miss deadlines). If your contractor falls behind that could be the beginning of a

cascade of problems and additional expenses that you may not (but should be) anticipating.

Be wary of contractors offering you much lower prices. Often, contractors will come in at a lower price, only to hike their prices later with change orders. Or, they use substandard materials or omit certain aspects of the job, in order to come in at a lower bid. Just remember you get what you pay for and it would be terrible to have to go back in later and fix lots of mistakes made by a previous contractor – mistakes that waste your time and your profits. When the work is finished, inspect the offices and create a punch list of any additional things that may need to be done by your general contractor.

Important Money Issues

Don't let operating costs in your new location surprise you, especially if you are moving to a new state. Find out what tax advantages or disadvantages you will have in your new (desired) location before making the decision to move there. Florida has no state income tax, but Virginia does, for example. See: https://taxfoundation.org/facts-figures-2017/ .

Florida does require you to pay 7% state taxes on commercial leases, which increases monthly rent costs considerably. Sales taxes for consumers are also higher in some states than others. See: http://www.salestaxinstitute.com/resources/rates . If your offices will be based in the same state as most of your customers, those customers that were previously exempt from taxes on out-of-state online purchases, may have to add that cost to their bill.

Make sure you research and consider all state taxes, franchise taxes, income taxes, business taxes, licensing fees, and any local costs that may be different in your new location and which will increase your expenses and even affect the cost of your goods and services to your customers.

TIP #20

Should You Keep Both Locations Running While You Move?

If you plan to keep both locations open simultaneously for at least 30 days you'll need to consider the impact on the company of the extra expenses (to maintain utilities/personnel/equipment, etc., in two offices). You'll also need to think about the stress on the staff (to have neither location with a full contingent of employees) and many other issues that may influence the way your business runs and handles issues. However there may be many reasons to keep the 2nd facility functioning, the most basic of which is if you can continue to provide your customers with the level of services they've come to expect with just one office open during the move? Also there are many other items to consider in addition to customer service and cost when thinking about keeping the old office open during the move. For example: FedEx does not have a "forwarding address service". As a result, customers requesting expedited exchange orders, manufacturers that did not update your corporate address promptly and other deliveries can get routed to your old location, causing a lot of headaches for customers and staff. The decision to keep both locations up and running should be based on a list of pros and cons to do both that should include:

✓ Cost of keeping both offices open

✓ Impact on customers to close old office during move

✓ Impact on vendors to close old office during move

✓ Logistics of keeping two offices open

✓ The question of how long you'd keep two offices open

✓ Employee impact and number of staff that would be required to keep services up and running in old office until the new office is opened and set up

TIP #21

Creating Realistic Timelines

Start planning your move approximately 10 to 18 months ahead of the desired move date, if you can. Starting early will save you money and provide you with a wider range of options in regards to your move. Create a timeline with milestones and keep in mind that it will start out very flexible and become more firm as you get closer to the date of the move. Expect the timeline to change and don't let it stress you out if you see that things aren't moving as expected – be prepared to be flexible and make changes along the way. Your timeline should be a starting point and SHOULD be flexible to accommodate changes and new issues as they arise. There are a lot of moving parts to any office relocation, so just use your timeline as a guide and adjust it as necessary as you move forward. If you are unable to plan that far in advance, do not worry, many smaller moves can take place on a tighter time schedule.

TIP #22

When is the Best Time to Move?

When determining the best time to move you'll need to consider the seasons, the economic or business influences that are specific to your industry, the optimal time of year and the best days of the week. Which month and what year is optimal for your business depends on what you do. If your business is brisk in the summer months you'll want to move in the winter (unless you live in the cold north). In that case you may need to compromise and move somewhere after the summer but before the onset of the cold weather. In any case depending on where you're located, the weather and your businesses' busy season you will want to adjust your move date accordingly.

Consider moving your company in phases if your business is very large. You could start on a Friday and move all the executive offices, then move marketing and sales on Saturday and save Accounting and Operations for Sunday (for example). No matter how you break it down, if your business is very large you may want to consider doing the move in phases to break up the work.

One company who hired us to help with their move had over 200 employees at a single location. For that reason we found it was easier and more economical to divide the move up and relocate them by department. The building management had a rule that tenants could only move after business hours or during weekends. We also had to consider the particular issues and schedule needs of each department. As a result, we moved 65 employees over the first weekend (the Sales Department), 136 over the following weekend (the Field Service Department), 41 employees the third weekend (from the Call Center) and then the remaining 33 employees the final weekend (including the Accounting Department and the company's corporate executives). Dividing up the business by department made the move easier and more organized and the company that we

TIP #22

were moving found it easier to keep business operations going without much disruption to their customer service or other operations.

If you own a retail business that does 80% of your sales during the Thanksgiving & Christmas holidays, you'll want to consider a move in the spring or whenever your business has the lowest activity. Other time-related things to consider include factors like when you do the bulk of your shipping (what time of year, what day of the week) and when your employees work (so you can get them to help you with the move). If you have additional staff that normally works over the weekends, for example, perhaps that would be an optimal time to schedule your move.

TIP #23

Creating a Relocation Budget

If you don't create a relocation budget, or feel that it is not an absolute requirement, what could happen? Typically, you'll end up mismanaging the money you've got to cover necessary expenses. A budget is the appropriate way to manage your money and to ensure that no aspect to "the move" is overlooked or left out. In order to stay on top of your relocation finances, you'll need to edit and update your budget on an ongoing basis.

What types of expenses need to be included in your budget? First, start with your project outline/plan making a notation about expenses as they relate to every item on the list. Notate if the expenditure is a onetime expense (such as the cost of the movers or the phone installation charge, etc.) or if the expenses are recurring (such as with operating costs like payroll & utilities or equipment leases).

Here is a sample list of expenses you'll need in your budget:

- ✓ Insurance

- ✓ Security deposit on new property

- ✓ Advisory fees for office relocation service providers & movers

- ✓ Professional fees (attorney, architect, CPA)

- ✓ Office design, build out and interior decorating materials

- ✓ Furniture & equipment

- ✓ IT & Telecom systems

- ✓ Existing office repairs

- ✓ Employee recruitment & relocation costs

TIP #23

✓ New stationery/letterhead, business cards, website, brochures, direct mail pieces, sales men's materials, product packaging, point of sale materials, customer catalogs and other marketing collateral.

Be prepared to update your budget frequently. Create a contingency because it is likely you might go over your budget even as much as double what you have estimated.

TIP #24

Planning Your New Office Space

When moving into new offices you typically fall into two categories. Either you are going to move into a space "as is" (or with minor changes) or you are going to gut the office and customize it to your needs.

If you are going to use a space "as is", then you will need to keep this in mind.

1. You don't know the condition of the network cabling or phone cabling

2. You don't know which power outlets and overhead lights are on which breaker.

Don't be that person who says "It'll be fine! Let's save the money and use what's already here!" At the very least you should map out the network cabling, phone cabling, power outlets and overhead lights and note how many of each are on each breaker or circuit BEFORE you sign the lease. If you don't have enough plugs or cables to accommodate your staff, adding them or rewiring them could end up costing you thousands of dollars in unnecessary expenses and extreme headaches for YEARS to come. I've seen companies lose money and face significant challenges because they didn't map out the cabling systems and breaker circuits before signing a lease and moving into an office.

If you're building your own building or renovating a new office space, then be sure to involve your IT staff or consultant with the build out. They will need to advise the HVAC, electricians and flooring installers to ensure that the proper measures are taken to provide for the network and phone equipment. Dedicated electrical circuits will be necessary for some equipment as well as appropriate cooling systems that need to be considered in order to prevent hardware disasters.

TIP #24

Once we had a client that had been in their new offices for several years before determining that the electrical on BOTH of their outer walls was not on their own circuit breaker box. They were actually using their neighbor's electricity during that entire time and while this may sound like a great deal to some of you – wait until you need to flip a breaker switch when it's after hours, only to realize it's locked in the office next door. In the case of our client, the only way they determined that they had this problem was when their neighbor moved out and disconnected their service, causing our client to lose a large portion of their electricity. An electrician had to be called in after the fact and this caused days of unproductive time for the business.

TIP #25

Consider The Services That Would Be Available In Your New Office

It's a good idea to review the list of service providers that currently serve the new offices you're considering BEFORE you sign a lease. The reason for this is that you can increase or decrease your spending in the area of utilities when you switch to different types of providers. If you have two new potential office spaces that are equally desirable, it would be a good idea to know if costs are going to go up dramatically at one location or another. The one way to determine this would be to compare costs at the different locations.

Ask the building management for a list of the utility suppliers that provide services to your potential new offices. Then get quotes from whatever providers are available at the new prospective properties. Read the quotes carefully to ensure you are quoting apples to apples. Do this before signing a lease because you'll want to get these quotes and compare the numbers before deciding which property you're going to take. It's always essential that you consider and compare all the costs for each property so you can be sure that you have an accurate budget forecast to base your decision on.

Keep in mind that if you are moving into a building with fiber optic service, for example, you will find that you can save money and get better service because fiber is extremely reliable and comparatively less expensive.

> **Author's Note:** Did you know that if you have a provider who you want to do business with, that doesn't appear to normally provide services in your new building, they will in some cases install their circuits for you? In some cases, construction fees may be incurred. However you can also eliminate those fees if you get other tenants to agree to subscribe to their service.

TIP #26

Preparing for the Day of the Move

Anyone helping with the move is going to need to have access to parking, the building and the office itself. Be sure to provide anyone who will be entering and exiting your new offices with keys and keycards and other entry and exit assistance information. Confirm that parking will be available and accessible to your employees during the move. If your new offices have restricted parking slots you may have to make special arrangements and get instructions about where to park during the move if that is prior to getting permanent parking instructions at your new facility.

If you've prepared site maps, team member lists (with phone/cell numbers) and other identifying signage, lists and maps – now would be the time to make sure they are hanging and visible by everyone involved. Don't forget to bring some tacks or tape that will allow you to hang these materials in the new offices.

There will be other little things that you'll need to prepare for on the day of the move that are often overlooked. For example if your moving van will need to stop in the street, you'll need to contact the police to let them know the date and time of your move so they don't ticket or even attempt to tow your truck.

If your old or new business has janitors, elevator attendees or door men (for example) you may need to make arrangements to have some tips available for your employees to give out to these people, especially if special favors will need to be asked of them.

If your employees are going to help you pack and move, then be sure to provide food and water for whoever is going to be helping with the move. There will be a lot of people moving around, carrying boxes, packing and unpacking – and all of this is work that your employees may not normally be expected to

TIP #26

do. So for that reason it's considered good manners for you to provide food and drink for everyone (and don't forget to offer water and beverages – at the very least – to your movers and consultants). Be sure to let your employees know that you're going to provide this in advance of the move so they don't bother packing up lunches for that day.

TIP #27

Using "the move" as an opportunity to update & improve your marketing

There are a large number of marketing elements to consider when moving your business. Any and all existing marketing pieces will have to be considered one by one to determine what will need to be done.

All your business communications materials will need to be updated and reprinted – things like letterhead, business cards and envelopes will, at the very least, need to be edited and reprinted. Since you have to reprint these items anyway, you may as well take this time to update these materials. If you have a competent marketing team or department, they should be used to short deadlines and handling things on their own, so depend on them to make this happen. If you don't have an in-house marketing team this would be a great time to consider hiring an outsourced marketing group. An "outsourced" team has usually worked "in house" or for a business before (vs. working for an agency) and so it's easy for them to figure out what needs to be done and get it done quickly, easily and without a lot of hand holding on the part of the person(s) managing the relocation or by anyone else.

In addition to your business communications materials you'll have to redo your brochures, catalogs, sales support materials, business plans, point of sale materials, digital marketing materials, websites, landing pages, html emails, retailer/distributor support materials and anything and everything that has your contact information on it. Depending on the size of your business, this can be a fairly big endeavor and it can be costly so you might as well refresh all your materials while you're at it. Again this is something you should be able to hand off to an "in house" or "outsourced" advertising team, but it will very likely be beyond the scope of an office manager or someone who doesn't have any advertising experience. Whoever handles it,

TIP #27

they should be able to manage the project with moderate input from you so you won't have to worry about spending a lot of time supervising this project.-

Don't forget that you may need a new sign in your new location. While it's unlikely that your old sign will match up with the specifications of your new office it wouldn't hurt to find out if it can be reused. Of course if you're revamping your advertising branding you may want to do the same with your sign to make sure everything looks fresh and new.

Another reason to consider refreshing your marketing materials now is because it's easy to combine a new "look and feel" with your announcement about your move. When a company moves it's often seen as a new chapter in a business' history, which piggy backs very nicely with the message that you've moved into a new facility. You can use this opportunity to play up the idea that you're moving out AND UP and on to better things. Your advertising team should be able to make a positive spin off of the move no matter what the underlying reason is for the change and use that as an effective business repositioning.

Consider having your ad team create a press release announcing your new move and submitting that release to local, regional or even nationwide media if that's applicable to your business. Make sure whoever does this for you knows how to get publicity for your type of business which involves creating and maintaining a list of media that might be interested in a story about your business. Tie this story into your social media campaign and have someone write a blog or a series of blog stories about how your new location will benefit customers or vendors or both.

It's really important to consider using a professional advertising team because [if they're any good], they should be able to make all this happen for just about any budget. A qualified

advertising pro should be able to save you significant amounts of money on things like your printing – opening up new budget amounts that can be allocated towards re-designing your materials. If you aren't experienced in this area you can lose more money making up for their mistakes than you'd spend by hiring a professional outside team.

At Your Business Solutions, we have a complete outsourced marketing department that has put together an exclusive offer for companies that are in the process of relocating. You can check this offer out here (it's really amazing): http://relocatingyourbusiness.com/the-marketing-department/

TIP #28

How extensive should your website changes be when you move?

Each year the Internet changes; the popularity of certain website design styles vary, browsers grow or fade in popularity, new search engine algorithms are released, new web marketing outlets develop, etc., so we believe it's important to keep your website and your web marketing efforts up to date as well. For this reason and others we think the issue of updating your website requires a tip of its own.

There are many reasons to update your website when you move. More and more users are using their mobile phones to view the web and most websites weren't set up to display correctly on a mobile phone. "55% of all time spent with online retail...occurred on a mobile device," finds web and mobile measurement firm comScore. (Siwicki, 2013) A new website should be "responsive" meaning that it should resize to fit any monitor or screen (no matter how big or how small). Your site should also be "mobile ready" meaning it should work properly in the iPhone and Android platforms and needs to be easier to use in that smaller environment. There just happens to be many reasons to update your web site now anyway, so you may as well discuss this with your IT crew or marketing people or hire an outside group to help you make this decision. You wouldn't want to invest any money to just edit the site if you could revamp it for just a little bit more.

Refresh Your Business Plan

Keeping your business plan up to date is one business strategy that rarely gets done, even if you don't decide to relocate. However, your finances, marketing strategy, and other crucial business considerations may be affected by your move and so it's best to take the time to update your business plan, both for the sake of organization and professionalism.

To do this, think about the ways your business might be affected by the move – will production capacity be increased due to new space to add additional production teams? Will sales forecasting need to be adjusted due to reduced sales during the month of the move? Will the marketing budget need to show an increase due to expanding printing costs for things like new checks, new signage or moving notices? Will shipping costs change due to the new location?

By making these important changes to your business plan, you'll be keeping this document up to date.

☒ TIP #30

Internal & External Communications
Throughout The Move

Incorporate a plan for internal and external communications. You need to have a steady flow of information back and forth between your in-house relocation team and your out-sourced vendors so that everyone knows what is going on and what is expected of them. Will you send out email memos to each team leader? Who will be responsible for disseminating the information to others outside your organization?

During and after a move you'll often find people are unsure of where to go or how to reach someone so as part of your communications plan consider creating a poster that you'll post in the new and old offices with the following information:

- ✓ All team members' cell phone numbers.

- ✓ All employees new phone numbers and/or extensions.

- ✓ All vendor names and contact numbers.

- ✓ The name and address at the new location.

- ✓ A contact name at the new and old buildings.

- ✓ The phone number for the old and new office management.

- ✓ A map showing the directions from the old office to the new one.

- ✓ One central contact name for a person responsible for issues and emergencies.

TIP #31

Upgrades Are Easier During Your Move

We've mentioned this before but it merits an entire tip because when you move that is also a very good time to evaluate the equipment that you have and replace it if necessary. You will often find that the costs on things like computers, copiers and phone systems have gone down since the last time you replaced those things. Also you'll discover that office systems are constantly being upgraded to improve employee productivity – so upgrading things like phone systems can reduce problems and increase the speed at which your customers are serviced, all contributing to the productivity of your staff and the bottom line. Sometimes you're forced to replace equipment at the time of the move because that's when it finally breaks down and stops functioning.

When you plan and implement a move you have many opportunities to interact with the people who use the company's equipment every day and to discover if there are issues or problems with the existing software and hardware. If your company is large, take this time to interact with your staff or fellow employees to ask them (by electronic survey, perhaps) if they are experiencing problems with any of their equipment and if they think they might be able to increase their own productivity with improved software and hardware.

In 2011, my company assisted a business who had a 17 year old digital phone system. They told us their plan was to operate in both the new location and the current location for at least 4 months. The issue we discovered was that the phone system manufacturer was no longer in business. Parts for their system would be hard to locate and if and when we found the parts, they would certainly be used. They relied on their phones heavily due to daily customer service requests, as many companies do. We suggested a Hosted VoIP solution to them which eliminated the need for space in the TELCO closet and enabled

TIP #31

them to simply unplug and move the phone when done. They didn't need to call a telecommunications vendor to come out and move the phones for them. Plus, since the new phones ran over the network, this reduced the number of voice/data drops by over 200 which saved them nearly enough to pay for the new phones.

Author's Notes: Moving old equipment is rarely a good idea. I cannot tell you how many times my technicians and engineers have serviced equipment that had been running for many years, but since the equipment was rarely powered off we were skeptical about it powering back on after a move. It's important to keep this in mind and don't blame your relocation team if a piece of equipment that's been running nonstop for 5 years stops working during a move. For this reason it's important to have a source of new or replacement equipment available and on standby in case anything needs to be replaced on an emergency basis. Everything has an expiration date but in the case of computer related equipment and other electronics, not everything has an expiration date stamped on the outside of it.

At Your Business Solutions, one our specialties is working with Telecom and IT systems. We have a really great phone system offer where you can actually get FREE handsets for your new office. Check out the offer here: http://relocatingyourbusiness.com/the-it-department/

TIP #32

Space Plans & Your General Contractor

Develop a space plan and office design with your **General Contractor.** Identify major tenant improvement projects and obtain permits. You should also begin working with your **Interior Designer** so you have a good idea of what you are going to need for an efficient and pleasant working environment. Talk with your employees to make sure you get their input on what they need to make their jobs easier and more productive. Make sure you discuss:

- ✓ Build-out requirements (walls, partitioning, storage)

- ✓ Refurbishment (painting, floors, blinds, lighting, ventilation)

- ✓ Restrooms

- ✓ Location (and size) of workstations & individual offices

- ✓ Location (and size) of reception, board & meeting rooms, employee lunch room, etc.

- ✓ Location for common IT equipment

- ✓ Other storage & equipment areas

TIP #33

Start Handling Some
Site-Specific Details

About nine months out you will need to:

✓ Evaluate server room and computer networking needs (or work with your **IT specialist** to handle these IT requirements)

✓ Identify phone system requirements (or work with your **Telecom specialist** to handle your telephone needs).

About six months out you will need to:

✓ Inventory all current furniture

✓ Inventory all office machines

✓ Address on-line, social media and web-hosting services

✓ Start working with your in-house marketing department (or an **Ad Agency** and/or **Marketing Company**) to develop, design and print new marketing materials

About three months out you will need to:

✓ Order new telephone & fax numbers

✓ Get your new telephone number as early as possible and arrange to get the number into the newest phone book, yellow pages and other phone related guides.

✓ Contact utility companies for disconnect/reconnect

✓ Order signage for the new location

TIP #34

Interior Designers Can Be Extremely Helpful When Relocating

Consider working with an Interior Designer on furniture requirements and purchases. A designer can help you to determine what old furniture and equipment you can keep, what can be refurbished and what needs to be replaced. You may want to hold an "office sale" to get rid of mis-matched furniture or equipment you no longer need. Alternatively you could offer employees an option on the furniture or donate and get a tax-deduction for your charitable contribution. Of course you can do this yourself but a designer has special skills to have you make your office more "work" and "productivity" friendly and often the added expense of hiring a designer is offset by the gains you'll make by having a more intelligent, workable office space. The designer can also help you to purchase new furniture as needed.

An interior designer can also help you to present your company in the best light. By helping you to create a professionally designed entry way, for example, your interior designer will help you with your marketing positioning (and help you promote your image to the outside world). By "thinking green" you can save money and help your environment. If you have any special furniture/equipment (such as artwork, antiques, mainframe computers, etc.) you may need to hire various **Office Moving Specialists** who have unique expertise in moving these types of items.

📦 TIP #35

Notify everyone who needs to know you've moved

Once you decide on your new location, make sure you send out notifications to everyone who needs to know that you have moved. This could be a sales & marketing bonanza by offering something to your customers since you need to notify them anyway. When you notify your clients that you're moving, take that opportunity to let your customers know that the move will not cause any interruption in their services or if it will, let them know the dates of your closure and what they can do if they have a problem during that time period.

Don't forget to send moving/change of address notices out to the:

- ✓ Post office
- ✓ Bank (don't forget you'll need to print new checks with your new address).
- ✓ Insurance companies
- ✓ Government agencies like the IRS
- ✓ Software companies
- ✓ All outside suppliers & vendors – be sure to tell all your vendors WHEN you will be accepting shipments at the new address.
- ✓ Carriers, ISPs and technology vendors
- ✓ Plant Caretakers – if you have a company that handles your plants call them to find out when they want to come to pick up and transport the plants in your office.
- ✓ Copier companies – confirm that it will be ok if you move the copier or if you need to have them move the copier to maintain the warranty. Ask for any special instructions about what may need to be done to secure the copier to

ensure you don't cause any damage to the machine.

✓ Customers – discuss when you're going to notify customers and make sure that employees know exactly what to say when they are questioned by customers.

✓ Make a list of the above vendors and customers and assign the task of following up for the next year after the move to make sure that everyone is using the correct (new) address information.

✓ Copier companies, vending machines, coffee companies or other vendors you buy supplies and lease equipment from.

✓ And don't forget that when you move your office you need to change your new address on your corporate registration paperwork.

✓ If you know far enough in advance where and when you're moving, you can send out your notices by 3rd class mail (bulk rate) and save a great deal of money on postage.

✓ Don't forget to confirm that the new management company is going to add your name to the company roster in the lobby of your new building.

Author's note: Use your social media outlets to inform customers about your relocation. Take this opportunity to stay in touch with your clients especially if you haven't done a good job of this before. Consider hiring an advertising agency to help you in this regard (and don't try to take on too much yourself). Your business' social media presence is often the first place many of your customers and prospective customers will turn to find out more about you, your business and certainly your business location. Failing to inform customers about your relocation, address and phone number can end up being a costly oversight.

TIP #36

Arrange to have desks, art & other equipment disassembled & reassembled

Contact a furniture assembler to come and disassemble your furniture and reassemble it at the new location. Perhaps this same person could be hired to remove white boards and artwork from your old facility and rehang it all at the new offices, because movers generally won't install these types of items. It's really important to get someone who knows what they're doing to do this because often the furniture is such that it doesn't easily reassemble once disassembled. Many tables, desks and files are made up of composite wood that essentially crumbles when someone tries to reassemble it- so do yourself a favor and hire someone who not only knows what they're doing but who will take responsibility for the equipment that you are trying to reuse.

TIP #37

Security Systems

Contact your security company to arrange to have the old security system taken down and reinstalled at the new office location. If a new security system is required be sure to plan far enough in advance to be able to get someone out to your new offices to inspect the facility, make a recommendation and provide you with a quote with enough time to get a system installed and operational before the day of the move. It's too dangerous to leave any of your artwork, electronics, technical equipment or other valuable goods exposed without any security for even one day. To learn more about security options click here: http://ybs.us/security-yes-or-no/

TIP #38

IT, Computers & Telecom
Decisions & Issues

Computers, phone systems and networks are the lifeblood of your office. Try to think back the last time your power went out or your network went down – was anyone able to work? Did any orders get processed or shipped? The answer to that is a resounding NO.

In this day and age orders can't reasonably be processed without your computers (and YES I suppose you could go get an old fashioned ticket pad and start filling those out by hand but I'm pretty sure that if you're selling widgets you're not going to want to send out a manual invoice with that next order). For that reason this is really one of the most critical aspects of your move if not THE most critical aspect of your move. It has to be done correctly and intelligently in order to avoid nightmares like added expenses and job delays.

It's absolutely essential that you prepare and plan for the moving of all your office equipment and correctly coordinate the timing of the setup of all your office systems (such as the networks, the Internet service provider, the phone systems, etc.). In the case of your computer systems, any missing element or service could mean the entire system wouldn't work and thus your employees and their work flow would come to a screeching halt. Check with your equipment warranties and service providers to confirm that moving that equipment yourself won't void the warranties.

TIP #38

Author's Note: In regards to furniture assembly, one problem that frequently occurs when an inexperienced team is handling a move, is when the furniture is assembled before the cables and electronics are run throughout the office. Make sure that if your furniture has to be assembled in areas that have power, phone and network connections, that you either leave enough space to reach the outlets or that the cables are fed through or under the furniture.

This forethought will eliminate delays and greatly reduce headaches for both the furniture assemblers and the IT/Telecommunications technicians. Planning the timing of the furniture assembly and the telecommunications/Internet installations in advance of any work being done, will make the move run faster and prevent employees from needlessly getting hurt when they try to move heavy furniture after it's been assembled and installed.

TIP #39

Consider hiring a professional IT team

Of all the different service providers you may need during a move, an IT group is possibly one of the most important to consider hiring (after the professional movers, that is).

The impact on your business, if your IT systems are not up and running when and where you need them, is too high and the results too detrimental to leave this issue to chance. Even if you have an in-house IT department, you may want to consider hiring an IT team that has specific experience relocating IT equipment. Make sure you do your due diligence and call for references when comparing your quotes. The least expensive company may not actually turn out to be the least expensive company when all is said and done. The costs associated with hiring the wrong company are easy to underestimate but when you think about it, a business without computers or phones is a business that comes to a screeching halt. Without your connection to the outside world, essentially no one can accomplish anything and your business will lose money.

Several years ago I worked with an oil company that had recently experienced a growth spurt and had planned to move to a larger office space. The lease had been signed and the planning stage was in progress for the move. After several meetings the company decided to take one of our competitor's bids for the same proposed solution because they were less expensive. The Friday they were to move into the new location I received a phone call from that company asking for help. It seems that only half of the contracted equipment was installed and they were told it would be weeks before it would be completed. We were able to pull our resources and had them up and functioning properly by Monday morning. The CEO personally thanked us and added that he will make sure due diligence is done for any future projects.

TIP #40

Backing up existing systems

Before unplugging one piece of equipment make sure that your systems are fully backed up and that they will be backed up to the very moment they are unplugged to be packed and moved to the new location. There are at least two good reasons to back up your systems 1) to record data in case it's lost during the move and 2) to retrieve information from an earlier date. Often referred to as the most essential element to any "Disaster recovery system", backup systems are absolutely critical for any business no matter how large or small.

A recent survey uncovered that 66% of people surveyed had lost files on their PC's. (Wikipedia) Setting up and managing a backup system can be complicated and this may be an area where you want to hire a professional to make sure you have a viable system in place before you move your equipment. A good backup system should include a testing procedure to ensure that the information you have backed up is intact, accessible and extractable. An IT professional knows how to properly validate the reliability of the data being stored and in the process ensure that your company can continue operations no matter what may occur during the move.

Don't take for granted that your phone system and servers will all power on without error or issues after a move. Our company was hired (after the client had moved) because the company had moved over the previous weekend. Sunday evening when they attempted to power up their systems, they did not like the results. The file server booted to an error. After their team troubleshot the issue for 9 hours they called us in panic at 10am Monday morning. We determined that they were using a tape backup system. Though they had nearly a month's worth of tapes, many of the backup tapes could not be read or were unable to be used to restore any files. This issue could have been avoided had they been more prepared.

TIP #40

Be sure to review your Disaster Recovery plan early on in your move planning process. If you determine that you don't have one, then don't be surprised if you end up being in the same situation as the company I just described.

There are several types of backup systems to choose from these days. The important thing is not that the system is being backed up; the most important element of a backup system is can the data be restored from your backups? Here are just a few questions to discuss with your IT Department manager or outsourced IT Pro:

- ✓ How are your systems backed up?

- ✓ How often are they backed up?

- ✓ Exactly WHAT is being backed up?

- ✓ How are those backups stored?

- ✓ How much time would it take to perform a FULL Recovery if necessary?

Your Business Solutions will provide a FREE Backup of your important files during your move. For more details on getting this critical backup taken care of, check out our FREE service and offer worth over $1000 here: http://relocatingyourbusiness.com/backup/

TIP #41

Working with your Contractors

Another issue that's important to consider before you unplug your first system is to consider how the "office build-out" will affect the installation of your technical systems. For example, installation of the network and phone cabling systems need to be coordinated with the furniture installations and build-out to prevent any unnecessary disassembly or reinstallations. So it will be important for you to interact with whoever is ordering new furniture or scheduling furniture reassembly to be sure your schedules coordinate with other service providers such as the IT and phone technicians. The last thing you need is to have one service provider do all their work only to find you needed to have them work together with someone else. Be sure to ask any service provider you schedule if they need to coordinate with any other providers. They should know better than anyone else if their work needs to coordinate with anyone else's.

Also, the wrong type of carpet can generate static electricity and can cause repeated crashes and reboots or even premature equipment failures to occur on servers and other computers. You'll want to work with your contractors (such as your interior designer & general contractor) BEFORE any carpeting is ordered to make sure that the carpets are designed to work with the technology systems in your office.

> **Author's Note:** Early in my career I worked for a nationwide copier company. I was assigned the senior technician's position for the sales location which employed roughly 100 people. Over the course of several months we had this one admin assistant who constantly had mysterious issues with her computer. After her first PC basically died (it wasn't even a year old) we replaced it. No more than 2-3 weeks later she started having issues again. I decided I was going to camp out near her desk every day until I could determine a pattern. Sure enough, by the second day I noticed that when she would

start having issues there was someone on the other side of the wall using the copier machine. The copier was on the same circuit as her PC. Every time it would start a copy/print job, it would cause a power "brown-out" on any device on that circuit. Her system was the only other device on that same circuit. We had a dedicated circuit installed for the copier and installed a battery backup (UPS) on her system to alert her if/when a power spike or brown out ever occurred again. This fixed her issue permanently.

⬙ TIP #42

Inventorying Your Existing Equipment

The project of moving an entire network system from one location to another involves a number of major steps, starting with an assessment and inventory of your current system. If you don't already have this written up for other purposes, now is an excellent time to create an in-depth inventory and map of your current set up. This inventory should include:

Create a list of all the equipment you have in use (as well as all the working equipment you have in inventory but that isn't currently being used). This list should include hardware, software, telephones, PC's, servers, printers scanners, etc., and list the item brand name, item functionality, model number, serial number, location item being used (or stored) (which should correspond to your department and office coding system and map mentioned previously in this book). Also be sure to inventory all cables, cords, UPS systems, connectors and other essential items like equipment manuals that will be needed to operate the gear. Make sure you describe how the connectors and cables are being used with each piece of equipment so that the item can easily be reinstalled at the destination. Note what type of power outlets are needed in each office, if they are not the standard, grounded 3-pronged outlet.

> **Author's Note:** A tip for collecting this system information is to contact your IT Department or IT Consultant. If they are using software to manage all of your systems, they should be able to pull a report with most, if not all, of this information. This one call could save you hours or even days of work.

TIP #43

Create A Central Repository For All Software And Hardware Passwords

Creating a master password list is something that should have been done before your move anyway, so if you don't have a list of all your software and hardware passwords you should create one now. All companies lose and gain employees and often when they do, they are faced with a number of serious problems resulting from hardware and software passwords not being shared with the company's IT department. It's better to set up a system in advance that will allow you to mandate what password systems and what types of passwords should be used in the business, but if you haven't done that at least keep track of what master passwords have been used so that you can access the employees files & systems once they are gone.

Instead of trying to guess what passwords past employees have used, consider setting up a "password management system" or software that keeps track of each employee's passwords. If you do, you'll just have to keep track of each employee's "master password". Then if the employee leaves you'll be able to log into their "password vault" and access any and all passwords they've used over their tenure with your company. These systems often generate complex passwords for the users that don't have to be remembered by anyone once the user is logged onto the master password system. For more information about using password management systems visit this website: http://www. pcmag.com/article2/0,2817,2381432,00.asp

Don't forget that there may be certain digital information (such as passwords) that may need to be accessible *during your move* and so if you store this information on a computer that won't be turned on until half-way through the move, you will be sorry. Many password management systems, such as "Last Pass" http://www.lastpass.com - keep each employee's password "vaults" on the cloud so you can access that information no

matter where you are or what computer you're using as long as you have their master password.

Keep this list of your "master passwords" on your mobile phone or on a hard copy list so you can access it during the move and as soon as when systems are brought back up on line.

Author's Note: Regarding gaining access to all the computers in your office if you don't know the passwords - all Windows based desktops have the ability to create multiple types of accounts on them (these are often referred to as profiles or user accounts). If you have a small network, your system may not be connected to a Microsoft Windows Server Domain. In which case you would only have what Microsoft considers as a Local Account. I recommend that the "local administrators account" be enabled on all company desktops and the password be standardized across all of them. The end user is never given this password as it is for admin purposes only. The user will have their own account to sign into so they can work.

However on a Microsoft Windows Server Domain, the network administrator account typically will be granted local admin rights so they will be able to sign into the system regardless of the user assigned to the computer. Even in this scenario, I recommend a standardized local admin password due to unforeseen issues - consider it a failsafe.

TIP #44

Creating Location & Equipment Maps

In addition to an equipment inventory, be sure to create a "site map" of the old location showing where all the current departments and offices are located. This "site map" will start out as just an office layout but will later be expanded to include multiple overlays or layers that will show things like equipment (PC's, phones systems, printers, etc.), furniture, art, filing systems and other items in use in the company. The map will be expanded, on an ongoing basis, to eventually include all equipment in use as well as very detailed information about what cables and connectors are being used and where they go. This map of the old office may seem like overkill, but it will dramatically help you when you get to the new location and are wondering where each item is supposed to go.

If you don't have the time to create this map yourself, then perhaps you can provide a copy of the basic site map to each employee and ask them to indicate what equipment they have and how it's connected within their own office. If each employee provides these details for their own equipment, then no one person will have to spend too much time inventorying and outlining the systems they have in use in their own spaces.

In addition to a map (or instead of if you don't have the time to create a map) you could consider creating a list of all the departments and offices, in the order that you want them to be moved from the old office to the new one. That way the movers will have an idea of where you want them to start first and what's most important to be set up and running first.

Keeping track of
equipment manuals

If you don't already have a file with all the corresponding instruction manuals (and warranty information, notes about usage, copies of original purchase receipts, etc.) now would be a great time to set one up. You can either create a file that manages and sorts all the manuals for the equipment in your office or you can tape (or otherwise connect) an envelope to each piece of equipment and insert all the corresponding information in the envelope (including instruction manuals, warranty cards, technical specs, service contractors/contact info, etc.).

There is no better time than during a move to organize all the little things that you've been putting off such as matching up each piece of equipment in your office with the applicable instructions and other support paperwork.

☸ TIP #46

Creating & Implementing Labeling Systems That Work

Once you have the site map created and your equipment inventoried it's time to label each item for easy and quick identification. Each piece of equipment and each cord, cable and connector used with a given piece of equipment should be inventoried and labeled so that if they are separated from the original item/office, they can easily be reunited with the corresponding equipment and routed to the correct area or department.

The equipment labeling system should not only list information identifying the apparatus' use and functionality, but it should also contain information that corresponds to the office and department where it was in use. Make sure that your labels are easy to locate, to read and to understand and that the codes you use make sense & corresponds with any other identification systems you may be using during this move. Be sure to create a legend for your coding system and make sure that the legend is easy to locate during and after the move by any and all people involved. You may want to consider printing the legend on the site map to be distributed to all moving team members for easy referral.

Note about box labels: When you go to create labels for all your boxes you'll most likely try to save time using sheets of labels and an inkjet or laser printer. If you're thinking of using inkjet printed labels keep in mind that the ink on inkjet printed labels tends to run if it gets wet, whereas the ink on laser printed labels does not run when wet. While you may not think that your boxes will get wet during your move, don't forget about Murphy's Law!

TIP #47

Determining If New Equipment Is Needed

Before moving on to the new office's maps and plan, you may as well take this time to determine if any new equipment is needed. You'll be interacting with each of your employees who may tell you at that time if something's not been working correctly or if something needs to be replaced.

Take this time to communicate with the employees involved and find out if things need to be upgraded (or perhaps just repaired). A network is only as good as each individual piece of equipment (computer, cable, router, etc.) and so to ensure your new network operates correctly; take this time to review what you need to replace to certify your new network systems work properly.

TIP #48

Assessing the New Office & Creating a New Site Map

Once you have your old office mapped out and equipment inventoried and labeled it's time to visit the new location. Your initial visit should include a review of the space that's been allocated for your server room as well as all the offices where the phones, PC's and other network equipment will need to go. Create a second site map of the new location showing all the company's departments and offices, making sure that you use the same identification system you used on your original site map discussed earlier in this book. That system outlined all the departments and offices in your company.

If you mapped out your old offices (showing each department and office in "map form") and if you inventoried your equipment and created a logical labeling system when you moved out of your old offices, then it should be easy to refer to any given location on the map of your new offices and discover what equipment goes where. If each piece of equipment is properly labeled, then you can tell where the item came from and where it needs to go.

TIP #49

Ensuring Power & Network Plugs are in Place

There's more to moving IT and phone equipment than moving equipment from "point a" to "point b". Once you get the equipment moved, in place and connected up to each other, you'll need to have the power and Internet connectivity to make them work. This task is essential to do BEFORE you move the equipment into place because it takes forethought to ensure that the systems are installed correctly and in the right location during the build-out phase of the move-in. Some electricians will offer to do your network and phone cabling for you. This is not recommended however, as these types of cables are installed differently by electricians than by IT professionals. If your electrician staples your network/phone cables, as they would your electrical lines, this could cause interference, a reduction in your data quality and cause noise issues on your lines.

It's also critical to ensure the related utilities, such as electricity, Internet connectivity and other data services are turned on when the employees move into place. The above mentioned site maps will help your general contractor to ensure that the proper cabling systems are in place before the drywall is hung and walls are painted. Alternatively, if you opt to hire an IT/relocation specialist they will create these maps and systems for you and handle everything from start to finish.

No matter who is handling the move of your IT systems, be sure to meet with them to discuss power & phone outlets as well as IT related service connections. Indicate on a fresh site map of the new offices, where you would like jacks to be installed and what types of connectivity you will need in each location. Remember to consult with each employee [if you can] to hear about their needs and to discuss how their office systems flow, to make sure you're asking for these jacks in the most optimal locations.

◆ TIP #50

Ordering Electricity, Phone And Network Services On Time

You're better off over estimating then under estimating the time you will need to get the office utilities/services ordered and operational. Most service providers should be called approximately 75 days prior to the move to allow plenty of time for the carriers and providers to get the orders processed and installed. For more specific timing information refer to the list below:

✓ **For electricity:** 30-60 days should be acceptable.

✓ **For Voice & Data circuits:** you should start evaluating the available circuits 120 days prior to activation. Submit signed contracts 90 days prior to move in. Confirm the physical installation address when signing the contract then confirm again at 60 days prior and again 30 days prior. The address is EXTREMELY important and can delay your staff from working the first day.

TIP #51

Testing All Services & Equipment Before They Need To Be Used

It's critical to allow enough time to test all the newly moved & installed equipment as well as the newly set up services before the staff is going to need to use their systems. This is one of the hardest things to plan for because there is often not much time between the date of the move and the date the employees want to start using their phones & computers. You may likely have to plan to work a weekend or overnight to be able to make sure that everything is functioning properly before they go into full use.

You may want to order overlapping services at both the old and the new offices. This will be especially important if your company plans to keep the old office operating while the new office is being set up and even more important if they want both offices to maintain a functioning customer service or other department. In that case, it becomes essential to keep the old services on while starting the new services at the new location. Keep in mind that you can ask the service providers (such as your ISP, your telecommunications service provider and your electricity provider) to provide special testing certifications on the lines to ensure that everything is functioning properly before the move in date.

In addition to installing, turning on and operating each piece of equipment you are moving, you may want to leave a survey form in each office to ask some of the basic questions about how the employees' systems are operating, in order to be able to quickly assess and service whatever systems need attention.

TIP #51

Author's Note: I cannot emphasize enough how important testing your equipment is before moving. Numerous times companies have been in a rush and failed to make time for testing. We have seen every possible failure from power outlets to security door access issues. Delegate this if you must, but only to a person who is responsible and thorough. Otherwise it is just as if you didn't test anything at all. You can find a downloadable checklist on our website www.relocatingyour-business.com

TIP #52

Consider A Cloud Based Phone System For Your Business

VoIP is a cloud-based phone solution. It lets you use your company's high-speed Internet connection as a phone line. If you have to relocate to a new location, or you're simply opening a new company branch, you can easily tie the new location into your existing VoIP network. As you're making the transition, you're guaranteed never to miss a call, since you take your business phone network with you on your smartphone. All of your devices are kept in the loop and in sync. Smartphones, tablets, desktop computers and laptops can all take advantage of your VoIP system, which means big changes to your company won't create big problems for your communication solutions.

There's enough hassle when it comes time to relocating and more than enough expenses. Taking one element of uncertainty out of the equation can go a long way toward alleviating growing pains for your business. With no out-of-pocket expenses for equipment, low monthly costs, and a host of advanced features, you're going to want to make VoIP a part of your next company move.

Learn more about cloud based phone systems here: http://ybs.us/your-technology-department/what-we-do-technology/tele-communications/

TIP #53

Which Is Better? A Self-Serve Move Or Hiring A Mover?

One of the major considerations when moving is deciding if you can handle the move yourself or if you should hire a professional mover to help with the job. If you have a large employee pool to draw upon for labor and your business isn't too big you may want to consider handling it yourself. Other than that, you'll want to hire a professional mover for many reasons. If your company fits into the "small business" category, you need to consider a lot of little details that would otherwise be handled by a mover. Things like truck rentals, dollies, boxes & packing materials, loading, employee liability (in case someone gets hurt lifting furniture) and many other things that you'd probably rather not think about will fall on your plate rather than that of the professional moving company.

If you're going to attempt the move yourself, make sure you review the rental agreement on the rental truck to determine if there are any limitations as to what can be moved in the truck and if you'll be charged for mileage & gas or if the truck can be dropped off at a location other than the one you picked it up at and what the insurance requirements will be.

TIP #54

Consider Container Packing
A.K.A. Crate Moving

"Crate Moving" is an option you may want to consider if you're going to have a delay between the time you need to clear out of the old office and move into the new one. Also referred to as "Container Moving," crate moving is also a helpful alternative if you aren't able to pin down an exact move out day. The container company can deliver the "pod" to you and you can move out of your office as quickly or slowly as you want to without having to do it all in one fell swoop.

Another good thing about container moving is the fact that you only have to load and unload them one time – so if you have a delay between the time you need to move out of "location a" and into "location b", you'll only have to pack and unpack the container one time. You just leave your furniture/files in the container until you're ready for them, reducing the amount of handling the items will have to undergo during the move and minimizing the opportunities for damage. Another benefit of container moving is that many of the container locations are air conditioned, providing the best environment for higher end furniture and art. PODS, one of the bigger companies that handles container moving, brings their pods to you, leaving them there until you call them to come retrieve when you are ready for them (PODS™ is a registered trademark of PODS http://www.pods.com/). Then if you don't want the containers to be delivered to the destination right away, they will store them until you need them to be retrieved, moved and delivered to your new location.

TIP #55

Should You Hire A Professional Packing Service?

Most people think they can handle their own packing but there really is an art to it, that when done correctly will protect your valuables and office contents in a way that nothing else can. There are several options to select from in regards to professional packing companies including "Full service" packers (that pack your entire office) or "Specialty packers" (who pack just a few select higher value items such as artwork, electronics or other specialty items that are harder to pack). It may cost more to use a professional packer but it's a great option when you have items that are expensive or particularly hard to replace.

Packing can be one of the biggest challenges of your move - especially if you have a large number of valuable items or if you plan on having your own (untrained/inexperienced) workers pack their own areas or departments. Whether you select professional packing services for your entire business or for just a few special items, you can get convenience and peace of mind while you reduce the amount of damage and issues you'll have when you finally reach your new facility.

TIP #56

Handling Your Own Packing

Avoid Moving Day disasters; as mentioned above, efficient packing is important and if you're going to handle your own packing there are some important tips you will want to consider:

- ✓ What you are packing and what type of box to use.

- ✓ If special packing materials are needed to keep an item from being broken or damaged.

- ✓ How to mark the box to make it easier to route to the correct location and to unpack.

- ✓ How to create an inventory of boxes for each department and for the entire office.

TIP #57

Packing Material Basics: Boxes

Purchase new boxes when you can and if you purchase too many keep in mind that many of the major box suppliers (like U-Haul) buy back unused boxes. If you don't have a budget to buy all brand new boxes, you can get sturdy boxes from local businesses but note that boxes lose their protective qualities the more they've been used so be careful to select only very sturdy boxes.

Some discount stores (like Wal-Mart) will give you access to their stores during stocking hours (11pm to 1am) where you can find many different sizes and types of boxes. If you use "used boxes" be sure they don't have any punctures and all the flaps are "intact" – if there are shipping labels on them cross those off with a marker to reduce confusion for the moving team. The big shipping companies (like UPS and FedEx) have tested boxes over the years and developed box strength specs that will help you to determine which size of box is appropriate for a particular item – to access this list online visit the UPS site at: http://www.ups.com/content/us/en/resources/ship/packaging/guidelines/how_to.html

TIP #58

Packing Material Basics:
Internal Protection

Purchase packing materials that are appropriate for what you're packing. There are many different types of packing materials from paper/newsprint to "peanuts" to bubble packing. If it's not obvious what materials to use, you can determine the correct packing materials for a particular item by visiting this web site where a variety of different protective materials are outlined: http://www.ups.com/content/us/en/resources/ship/packaging/guidelines/how_to2.html

TIP #59

Organizing Your Packing Materials & Training Your Personnel

Set up separate areas in each department where packers can access packing materials. Hold a training session prior to the move to teach your employees how to pack a box. Make sure each employee knows:

✓ Tape the bottom of each box and use a box that is sturdy enough for the item they are packing.

✓ Don't over pack a box and make it so heavy that it's difficult to carry. Pack heavy items (such as books) into smaller boxes.

✓ If a box holds a heavy item be sure and label is as "heavy" so the movers don't get injured trying to lift the heavy box.

✓ Use "bubble wrap" or "packing paper" to pack fragile items and be sure to mark those boxes as "fragile".

✓ Each office should have at least one box of "essentials" that is marked as such that can be spotted and opened as needed when they get to the new office. The goal should be for each employee to get their work areas up and operational as quickly as possible.

TIP #60

Organizing & Identifying Boxes & Equipment

Be sure to set up a labeling & numbering system (as previously mentioned) and then label/number each box appropriately. For example, one office may have a total of 5 boxes and each should be numbered as follows:

- ✓ **"Office A1 Box 1 of 5"** (with "A" being the designation for a particular department and "1" being the number of an office within that department).

- ✓ A list or a photo of the contents of each box should be taped to the side of each box for easy identification. Optimally a copy of this list should be kept aside and collected to become part of a master list.

Your labelling system will ensure that all the contents and boxes for each office or department are easily accounted for. All boxes should be labelled with the origination and the destination information so it can be properly routed. An inventory of all boxes should be kept separately so that you know which boxes contain what (when you start searching for things, which you will) and to determine if any are missing.

When unpacking, check off items against this inventory list which was made at the packing stage. That way, should any item be missing or damaged, the movers can quickly be notified and you will know which items are missing (and ultimately which items need to be replaced, if the box contents are irreparable or never located).

Archives and current files also need to be properly marked and easily identifiable for proper placement in the new offices as well. Purge unneeded files so you're not trying to store excessive amount of data in your paper filing system. Send files you

have to keep but don't need on-going access to, to an offsite storage facility if possible.

If you're disassembling equipment and other furniture be sure and label those pieces so they can reassemble them at the destination office. If there are screws and little pieces that could easily get lost, be sure and put those in a zipper type bag, label the bag (in case it is separated from the equipment it goes with) and tape it to some related piece of the equipment so you don't lose them.

TIP #61

Keys To File Cabinets & Desks

Any keys for desks or filing cabinets should be labeled and taped to the equipment they correspond with. If you have a second set of keys (most filing cabinets originally come with a set of two), be sure to keep one master key chain with each key labeled and kept in a secure area in case the other keys are lost during the move.

TIP #62

Protect Valuables From Prying Eyes

You may want to consider packing up valuables and moving them yourself if you have any items that are of particularly high value. If this is the case, you may want to do this when less outside workers or employees are around to see what you're doing. In one instance a business stored a large amount of gold and silver coins inside their facility and since no one knew what was in the boxes, they thought it was safe enough to have the professional movers move the boxes during the move. However the boxes were not that large but they were extremely heavy for their size. So their relocation specialist advised against letting anyone other than top management touch those boxes, in order to prevent suspicion and eventual possible theft of the boxes at some point during or after the move. Consider packing up and moving those high value items separately. While you would never want to hire an uninsured or un-bonded moving company, you still don't want the things you hold most dear to disappear during the move.

DURING THE MOVE

TIP #63

Be Prepared For The Unexpected

The act of preparing to move your office essentially forces you to get ready for most eventualities, however unexpected events and issues still arise no matter how prepared you are. Here are a few examples of unanticipated issues you may want to prepare for:

✓ **Supplies** - Making sure you have enough supplies – especially if you plan on working after normal business hours when things like packing tape, RJ11 wire or a screwdriver might be harder to find at 1am in the morning.

✓ **Planning** - Many companies stop normal operations during a move but if you're going to attempt to keep an office up and running during the transfer, you'll want to try to think thru all the things that your "X Team" will need to make this happen....even things that they might not normally need but that they'd want to have access to in order to handle all the various types of customer requests.

✓ **Keys** - If your new and existing offices require key cards to get in and out of the facility you may want to ask for an extension of the time allotted for the cards to work, in case you need to return after the date you anticipate being out of the office.

✓ **Air Conditioning** - If you plan on moving during hours that are not considered "regular," you might need to ask to have the air conditioning turned on AFTER hours (or heat, depending on what time of year you're moving). Be sure and request this far enough in advance of your move

TIP #63

because some facilities systems are computerized and require any requests like this to be submitted far enough in advance to get the correct personnel to handle it.

What happens if you need to make copies but your copy machine hasn't been set up yet or you need to check your email but your server isn't functioning? These probabilities force you to think through all the processes related to your work and the move, to take nothing for granted and to attempt to anticipate the unexpected.

TIP #64

Create a "Do Not Pack" Zone

Save certain items for personal transport that are either high value or things that you will need the minute you get to your new location – items such as calendars, phone numbers (with moving team members' contact information), customer lists, computers that will be kept on during the moving process or other items with important information that may be needing DURING the move would be important to set aside. Certain office supplies, such as pens, dry erase board and markers, legal pads, and other things that can help you get organized would be helpful to move yourself so you have immediate access to them.

AFTER THE MOVE

TIP #65

The Simple Things That Often Get Overlooked

Some of the most fundamental final steps in moving a business are often forgotten, causing all sorts of problems.

For example, you should not forget to:

✓ Hire a cleaning company to clean your old office.

✓ Do a 'walk thru' of your old office checking in every built in cabinet and closet for things you've left behind. (don't leave anything behind by the way or your old landlord may charge you for its removal).

✓ Turn in all your keys to the old office/warehouse and any other storage areas, etc., including the mail box keys.

✓ Collect mail from the old mail box before leaving and make sure the mail forwarding order has been placed.

✓ Make sure all your utilities and services have been disconnected at the old office.

✓ Don't forget any storage areas in your old office building – if you've been storing an old desk in the basement now is the time to get it or ditch it.

✓ Make sure you collect any equipment that might be overlooked in the IT or Server room such as old phone systems. Even if you're not going to use an old system you need to remove it and dispose of it or sell it.

TIP #65

✓ Leave your contact information with a friendly neighbor in case one of the shipping companies tries to deliver a package to your old address (as mentioned before, Fed Ex and UPS don't automatically forward shipments so it's important to time your vendor and customer notifications correctly....and even if you do that sooner or later someone is going to ship something to your old address so it's better to be prepared).

✓ Ensure that your old phone number has a recording on your old line that will redirect callers to your new phone number. Make sure that the recording is in place for at least 6 months from the date of your move.

✓ Have a plan to get rid of empty boxes and used packing materials.

✓ Schedule employees to remove tags and labels from all their equipment and set up their own offices and desks.

✓ Schedule a team to install the supply room and break room to get the office to be fully operational as soon as possible.

✓ Make sure your have arranged to have the old office inspected and your security deposit returned.

TIP #66

Take the time to revamp
your call center

Moving is a great time to upgrade some of the services you provide to your clients or many of the internal systems & equipment that your business uses to operate each day. When you're moving, your systems & equipment are taken down anyway so you may want to reorganize or at least review those systems before recompiling them.

One of these systems is "customer service" and move time is a great time to revamp those related systems. It's always important to keep up with the latest customer service trends because if you don't, you know your competition will. With so many competitors using overseas providers to handle their customer service however, it's not hard to excel at great customer service if you're starting with native English speaking service providers. Studies indicate that as many as 70% of customers will buy products and services from companies with excellent customer service reputations. So when you're moving, take a little time to review and revamp your phone management systems & equipment as well as your processes and procedures that will provide you with fewer busy signals, better call response times, fewer call transfers and a multitude of new feature options provided by the latest phone systems available.

To learn more about revamping your call center visit http://ybs.us/your-technology-department/what-we-do-technology/technical-support/

TIP #67

Editing/Deleting your old business listings

Once your business has been relocated, create a list of your "Professional" business directories where you have a professional listing (for example, *Psychology Today* [therapists], *ABA Journal* [attorneys], *Modern Contractor* [contractors], and so forth. You can update your new address and phone number with these journals and associations by email or mail.

Do the same if your business is listed with your local Chamber of Commerce, BBB, or other places online where you control your listing or pay to have your business listed. Important directories you will be able to edit are Google, Yahoo, Yelp and yellow-pages.com.

Claim and edit these listings to reflect your new contact information and be sure to update employee or contact names while you're at it. Search for where you might be listed by doing a web search for: {business name, city, street} or {business name, city, street, old phone#}. Click on your business listing to see if there is an "Edit this listing" or "This business has moved or closed" button. If so, mark your business appropriately.

You may not want to do any more extensive editing but while you're there if you notice any negative reviews or customer comments you may want to take an extra minute to at least create a list of them in order to address them in the future.

TIP #68

Don't Delete Your Old Business Listings in Google Places or Directories Just Yet

If you rely on new business from your search engine listings and you are ranking well, it might be better for your listing to be incorrect yet visible than not visible at all. Without deleting your old listing, add your new listing with your new address in Google and the directories.

By the way, you can only add a new listing if you have a distinct phone number for it. You may need to explain to your new clients/customers that your office/store has moved, but a lost new customer might be better than nobody knowing where you are. Some relocated businesses put graphics on their websites' home pages & contact pages announcing their new locations, while still having their old listing & location remain a page 1 traffic driver to their website (they kept their old address in very small print in the footer of their website so Google could find it.)

Combine a Grand Opening Party With Your Moving Announcement

A corporate grand opening or client/vendor party is an excellent method to let people know you've moved. Plus you can generate new business from your existing (or previous) customers, as well as attracting new clientele at the same time. You could even combine your "moving" announcements with an event invitation and kill two birds with one stone and be sure to invite all your new neighbors as you never know who might be a potential client.

Consider having a custom-printed moving announcement created and make sure it matches the rest of your advertising campaign so you will benefit from having your existing and new customers see your corporate branding one more time. If appropriate for your business, schedule the event with the Chamber of Commerce and/or have ribbon cutting, special attendees, sales/specials, food & beverages and anything else that makes it a festive party.

Advertise online, make an announcement via all of your social media venues and through your website and partners' websites, send out email blasts or make telephone calls to your special clientele. Use your existing customer AND vendor database and supplement that by purchasing lists of clients that match your existing "best customer" demographic. Lists of potential clients can be purchased by any number of reputable online list vendors such as Info USA at http://www.infousa.com/ .

TIP #70

What Else Do You Need To Do To Host An Open House?

Most business owners host an open house in order to generate more access to the community and to introduce their companies to new potential clients. So when you move, the timing is right to combine these goals with the goal of notifying your existing customers and vendors of the new location. Let's take a closer look at what it takes to plan and host an open house at your business.

Hosting a successful open house requires a lot of planning and preparation. Begin by deciding what day you would like your open house to be on. First make sure you plan your open house *after you have finished moving* into your business space and after renovating, decorating, and placing all of your furnishings where you would like them to be. This shows guests attending your open house that you're in fact open and "ready for business". Be sure to give yourself enough time to actually plan the event.

Next, you need to establish a target audience and find affordable ways to market and advertise your open house. Keep your ultimate goal(s) in mind for having an open house.

Give yourself a projected budget for the open house and make a list of all the things you will need to conduct a successful event. If you want your employees to help in the planning and preparation process, make sure you calculate their wages or salary into the estimated budget. Estimate the costs of entertainment, food, marketing and advertising such as the cost of flyers, promotional items and gifts you plan to give your guests for attending the event.

☁ TIP #70

Planning your refreshments station is a task in and of itself. Since most people come to an open house event simply for the food, food is by far one of the most important elements essential to having a successful event.

Make your job easier by having a local restaurant or catering service provide the food and if you can afford it, hire a party planner to handle the entire event for you. If you hire a popular local caterer or restaurant, consider mentioning their name in your open house announcements as an enticement to getting maximum attendance. You may even do a co-marketing event with the restaurant which could help to share costs and introduce your business to their clients (and vice versa).

Give your guests an opportunity to learn about the products or services your business offers. If you want to feature your key products at your open house make sure they are either centrally located or in attractive display cases. If it makes sense, give out samples of your products during your open house because it gives guests a chance to try the product without spending any money. Whether you have a service or a product business, you can benefit by setting up booths, tables, or stations where you can feature brief service or product demonstrations.

Take this opportunity to display and distribute your newly revised marketing materials as that not only gets your name out to potential new clients but it also helps to reestablish your brand with existing clients.

CONCLUSION

A move can be a daunting task, and the size of the project will vary dramatically depending on how much furniture & equipment you have to move as well as how many employees you have that can help you. Many companies underestimate the amount of work required to keep their businesses running profitably at the same time as they're literally unplugging everything and moving down the street or across country.

The best way to avoid headaches and to get the job done economically and on a timely basis, is to start off with a comprehensive plan, invest time (and energy and money) into the pre-move preparation and whenever possible to hire professionals to help in those areas that you don't have the expertise to properly handle yourself. The tips in this book will help you to anticipate all the big and little things that companies sometimes overlook and help you to get through the moving process successfully and economically.

As a way of thanking you for making it to the end of this book, I've added some very special BONUS TIPS that every business will benefit from that you can view here:

http://relocatingyourbusiness.com/bonus/

If you have any questions or would like me or my company to assist you at any point during your move, please don't hesitate to contact me, Clint Brinkley, at 713-589-3111 or email me at clint.brinkley@ybs.us

YOUR BUSINESS SOLUTIONS has over 12 years of experience in the business services industry supporting companies with outsourcing needs in Accounting, Marketing, Tech Support and Sales Support with a special focus on helping companies to relocate their businesses.. For more information please visit: http://ybs.us/